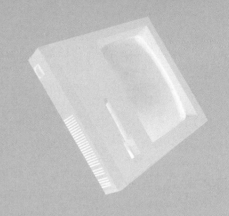

Computers

GREAT INVENTIONS

Computers

STEVEN OTFINOSKI

Marshall Cavendish
Benchmark

New York

To Dan, who is always there to help me with my computer.

Marshall Cavendish Benchmark
99 White Plains Road
Tarrytown, NY 10591-9001
www.marshallcavendish.us

Library of Congress Cataloging-in-Publication Data

Otfinoski, Steven.
Computers / Steven Otfinoski.
p. cm. — (Great inventions)
Summary: "An examination of the origins, history, development, and societal impact of the computer"— Provided by publisher.
Includes bibliographical references and index.
ISBN-13: 978-0-7614-2597-7
1. Computers—Juvenile literature. I. Title. II. Series.

QA76.23.O75 2007
004—dc22
2006030372

Series design by Sonia Chaghatzbanian

Photo research by Candlepants Incorporated
Cover photo: Corbis

The photographs in this book are used by permission and through the courtesy of:
Corbis: Daniel Attia/zefa, 2; Hulton-Deutsch Collection, 8; Bettmann, 12, 16, 19, 22, 24, 27, 90-91; Stefano Bianchetti, 15; Michael Nicholson, 21; Doug Wilson, 47; Gregor Schuster/zefa, 56; Louie Psihoyos, 57, 73; Kim Kulish, 62; Boris Roessler/epa, 64; Peter M. Fisher, 66; George Logan/zefa, 70; 74, 77; Reuters, 80; Patrik Giardino, 82; Adrianna Williams/zefa, 85; Jerry Cooke, 30-31; Roger Ressmeyer, 40-41. *Science and Society Picture Library*: 10, 34, 87, 88. *Art Resource, NY*: Scala, 14. *Getty Images*: Time Life Pictures, 39, 49, 51, 53; Catrina Genovese, 59; 36. *Computer History Museum*: 44, 76.

Printed in Malaysia
1 3 5 6 4 2

CONTENTS

GREAT INVENTIONS

Computers

EARLY COMPUTERS, SUCH AS THIS ONE IN A FACTORY IN MANCHESTER, ENGLAND, WERE ENORMOUS AND LIMITED IN FUNCTION. THIS ONE WAS KNOWN AS THE ELECTRONIC BRAIN.

From the Abacus to Engines

No invention of the last one hundred years dominates our lives as much as the computer, in all its various forms, does. We use computers to do our schoolwork, to provide us with information, to entertain us, and to communicate with one another. Computers perform all these functions with a speed and accuracy that is breathtaking.

Computers are so much a part of our lives today that it is difficult to imagine how we could live without them. And yet the modern computer is a relatively recent invention. Most adults older than forty can remember a time when computers played little or even no part in their daily lives. The first modern electronic computer did not appear until 1946. The Internet's World Wide Web did not exist before 1990. The personal computer did not become widely used until the early 1980s and did not evolve into the indispensable household tool it is today until the late 1990s. Yet scientists and mathematicians have been struggling to create machines that would compute or perform mathematical calculations since at least the seventeenth century. The history of the computer is filled with stubborn inventors, dreamers, schemers, and brilliant nerds.

The First "Computers"

The word *computer* comes from the verb *compute,* which means "to determine by calculation." Calculation involves primarily the adding, subtracting, multiplying, and dividing of numbers. For thousands of

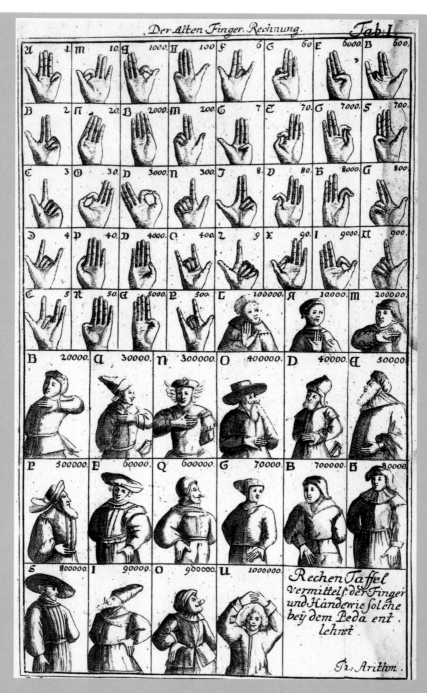

FINGERS WERE THE FIRST TOOL FOR MAKING COMPUTATIONS. THIS CHART OF A DIGITAL COUNTING SYSTEM WAS PRODUCED IN 1724.

years, humans have been looking for ways to make these mathematical processes easier to perform.

The first tool used to compute was, not surprisingly, people's fingers. Prehistoric hunters could tally the animals they killed on their fingers and hold them up to show their friends. But with only ten fingers, this method of calculating was limited. Once humans developed more complex societies that traded and bought and sold goods, a better tool for calculating increasingly sophisticated or complex transactions was needed.

The ancient Egyptians and Babylonians developed counting boards with grooves that held small stones or other objects. The Romans further refined the counting board using colored pebbles to perform calculations. Each color had a different value. For example, a yellow pebble stood for one. A blue pebble represented ten and a green one, a hundred. Using different combinations of pebbles, Roman businessmen could accurately perform calculations on their counting boards with surprising speed. The Latin word *calculus*, which today means a branch of higher mathematics, originally meant "pebble" or "stone."

Enter the Abacus

The Romans' colored pebbles proved effective to a point, but they were not uniform in shape and size and could be awkward to use. Eventually they were replaced by human-made beads, all roughly the same size and shape. Then about 1200 C.E., the abacus came into use in Asia. *Abacus* is a Latin word derived from the Greek word *abax* or *abaken,* meaning "table" or "tablet." This device, invented by the Romans, consisted of a rectangular wooden frame with several wires or grooves running across it. On each rod or groove were a number of beads. Each row of beads had a different value, like the Roman pebbles—ones, tens, and hundreds. The Chinese abacus, the most popular of these devices, had thirteen columns of beads divided by a crossbar. The values of the beads rose from the right to the left, beginning with one and going all the way to trillions. By moving the beads across the rod from one side to the other, a

THE CHINESE DID NOT INVENT THE ABACUS, BUT THEY DEVELOPED IT INTO A SOPHISTICATED CALCULATING MACHINE THAT IS STILL IN USE TODAY.

person could perform an array of calculations—not only the four basic mathematical operations but also more complex functions.

The abacus marked a significant advance in computing tools. It was self-contained, easy to operate, and portable. Variations of the abacus appeared in Egypt, Japan, and other parts of Asia. Use of the abacus spread to the Western world as well. Abacuses were still being utilized widely in China and Japan until the 1960s, a testament to their accuracy and usefulness.

Logarithms and the Slide Rule

The Middle Ages were a time of great learning in the West, but not in the sciences. Christianity, the predominant religion in Europe, viewed science, with its focus on objective human observation, as a threat to faith. By the seventeenth century and the onset of the Renaissance, the tide shifted, as important thinkers began questioning old beliefs, giving rise to a new age of reason. Many branches of science, including mathematics, flourished. Among the goals that inventors and scientists set for themselves was finding a better, more efficient way to perform mathematical calculations.

Logarithms, like pebbles or beads, were symbols that represented different numerical values. Only logarithms were in the form of written numbers. One equaled ten, two equaled one hundred, and so forth. Logarithms had been conceived of by mathematicians in ancient India about 200 B.C.E. But it was not until 1614 that John Napier, a Scottish mathematician, systematized logarithms into a table to make them easier to use. Napier's logarithm tables had a profound effect on mathematical calculation. They were still being taught in American high schools into the 1970s, when the electronic calculator largely replaced the need for them.

In 1621 English mathematician William Oughtred invented a tool that would calculate logarithms automatically. He put together two pieces of wood with logarithms printed on them and called the device a slide rule. By sliding the individual bars across each other and lining up the particular markings, the user could find the correct logarithm. Your

THE RUSSIAN MERCHANT IN THIS PAINTING BY BORIS KUSTODIEV SEEMS AS PROTECTIVE OF
HIS ABACUS AS HE IS OF HIS MONEY.

grandparents probably used slide rules in school to perform more complicated math problems.

Mechanical Calculating Machines

As technology continued to develop in Europe, more and more mathematicians were creating machines to perform calculations. In 1623 German scientist Wilhelm Schickard came up with a machine with sprocketed wheels that used Napier's logarithm tables to add, subtract, multiply, and divide.

The French mathematician and philosopher Blaise Pascal invented a more substantial mechanical calculator in 1642. Pascal's calculator was the size of a shoe box and used a series of gears and levers to add and subtract numbers. When the "ones" wheel had turned all ten numbers on it, making a complete revolution, the "tens" wheel to the left went up one notch, and so forth. Pascal's invention was the great-grandfather of the modern odometer, used to record mileage in automobiles.

Pascal built fifty copies of his Pascaline, as he called it, and sold them to wealthy patrons. However, they were too expensive to be practical. Another problem with the Pascaline was that it could only solve the simplest of math problems.

BLAISE PASCAL WAS MORE THAN THE INVENTOR OF ONE OF THE FIRST MECHANICAL CALCULATING MACHINES. HE WAS ALSO A MATHEMATICIAN, A PHILOSOPHER, AND AN AUTHOR.

GERMAN GOTTFRIED VON LEIBNIZ, WHO IMPROVED ON PASCAL'S CALCULATING MACHINE, WROTE BOOKS AND ESSAYS ON EVERYTHING FROM MATHEMATICS TO POLITICS TO HISTORY.

In 1673 German mathematician and philosopher Gottfried von Leibniz improved on Pascal's machine with his Leibniz wheel. This large machine could add, subtract, multiply, and divide. But Leibniz's greatest contribution to the computing machine was the creation of a numerical system that reduced all numbers to combinations of zero and one. This binary system, which Leibniz wrote about in a 1701 essay, was further developed in 1854 by English mathematician George Boole and would become the basic code for all modern computer languages. Each 0 and 1 making up a sequence of the numbers would be called a bit, a basic unit of computer information, and a group of eight bits would become a byte.

Punch Card Computing Machines

Throughout the eighteenth century, Leibniz's contemporaries continued to look for simpler ways to make calculations. With the dawn of the Industrial Revolution in the 1700s, inventors found new uses for computing machines. In 1728 Frenchman Robert Falcon punched holes in a card to match the position of warp threads in a loom. Each row in the weaving pattern had its own punch card, and each hole in the card corresponded to a particular warp yarn in that row. The holes in the cards either raised or depressed the warp, causing the loom to work.

In 1801 another Frenchman, Joseph-Marie Jacquard of Lyons, refined Falcon's punch cards so that a loom could be "programmed" to weave different patterns. The Jacquard loom earned the praise of the Emperor Napoléon. But the weavers of Lyons saw Jacquard's invention as a threat to their livelihoods, and he was forced to flee the city. Nonetheless, his loom became a great success and is still in use, in a more updated version, today.

Father of the Modern Computer

About 1820 English math professor Charles Babbage took up the challenge of creating a better computing machine. Babbage was frustrated by the inconsistent French math tables he was using to perform calculations. He conceived of a sophisticated computing machine he called a difference engine, a device composed of thousands of gears, wheels, and tiny metal rods that made contact with the punch cards. For about fifteen years Babbage labored on his ambitious invention, and early on completed a small working prototype. But fashioning the intricate and complex parts of a larger working model was beyond the ability of contemporary craftsmen.

Dismayed but undaunted, in 1834 Babbage took yet another approach to developing the analytical engine. His proposed machine would be able to perform all kinds of mathematical operations and print out the results. The analytical engine would use punch cards to store the memory of a particular program. This concept proved to be the foundation of the modern computer. But Babbage, who had a cantankerous personality, alienated the people who could help finance his ambitious project, including the British government, which withdrew its funding after nineteen years without any tangible results realized. Even if Babbage had been able to raise enough money for his device, it is unlikely that craftsmen could fashion the 50,000 separate moving parts his grand machine required.

Babbage had more successful ideas, such as conceiving the cowcatcher on the front of locomotive trains and devising the actuarial table that first accurately assessed human life expectancy. He also helped to found the Royal Astronomical Society. But at the time of his death in 1871, Babbage's efforts to create an advanced calculating machine were all but forgotten.

A Census Machine

In 1884, fifteen years after Babbage's death, an American inventor named Herman Hollerith combined a punch-hole system with the newly harnessed power source of electricity to create the first electromechanical computing machine.

Hollerith had a specific purpose in creating his machine. Every ten years the U.S. government conducted a census. The process of tabulating the results by hand was slow and painstaking. It often took the

ENGLISH MATHEMATICIAN CHARLES BABBAGE, SHOWN IN AN UNDATED PHOTOGRAPH, CONCEIVED THE FIRST MODERN COMPUTER.

The Countess and the Computer

If Charles Babbage failed in his work with computers, it was in spite of the effort of a woman who proved his greatest advocate and one of the finest female mathematicians of her time.

Augusta Ada Byron was the only daughter of the English romantic poet George Gordon Byron and Anne Isabella Milbanke, a pioneering woman mathematician in her own right. Ada inherited her mathematical ability from her mother and her writing ability from her father. A keen student of math, Ada met Charles Babbage through a mutual friend. She became intrigued by Babbage's analytical engine and translated a French article about it into English. Babbage admired her ability to understand his invention and admitted that she could describe it in words better than he could. "The Analytical Engine," she wrote poetically, ". . . weaves algebraic patterns, just as the Jacquard loom weaves flowers and leaves."

Ada married a man who later became the earl of Lovelace, making her a countess. They had three children, but she never abandoned her passion for Babbage's computing machine. She created a series of instructions enabling the computer to perform a task. It was the world's first computer program. Like the engine itself, it was never implemented. Ada's last years were troubled. She became addicted to gambling, losing increasing sums betting on horse races. Then she contracted uterine cancer that took her life at age thirty-six.

Her unique role in the history of computers, however, was not forgotten. In the 1970s the U.S. Department of Defense named a computer language Ada in her honor.

Anne Isabella Milbanke, mother of Augusta Ada Byron, was also a pioneering mathematician. Her marriage to the poet George Gordon Byron ended soon after Ada's birth.

THE COMPANY THAT HERMAN HOLLERITH FOUNDED IN 1896 TO TABULATE NUMBERS EVENTUALLY BECAME INTERNATIONAL BUSINESS MACHINES (IBM).

entire decade from one census to the next to record the results. Hollerith hoped his "census tabulating" machine, could speed up this process.

Three years later he made an improvement to his computing machine. He took a card and punched holes in it to record and represent each piece of key information related to a given individual—including the person's age, sex, and occupation. The card was then placed in a slot in his machine. More than two hundred tiny pins on a metal plate pressed down on the card. When the pins that matched up with the holes passed through the card, they made contact with a bath of liquid mercury beneath it. This completed an electric circuit that powered a needle on a dial, advancing it one notch and adding one more person to the total count for that category. When all the cards were processed, the operator of the tabulator could then read the final counts recorded on the dials.

Some fifty-six of Hollerith's machines were bought by the U.S. government and used in the 1890 census. Information on more than 62 million Americans was processed in a mere six weeks, saving U.S. taxpayers five million dollars in operating costs. Hollerith became so successful that he established a company to manufacture calculating machines in 1896, calling it the Tabulating Machine Company. The company merged with two other companies in 1911 and assumed the name International Business Machines (IBM) Corporation in 1924. Today IBM is the largest maker of computers in the world.

Hollerith's tabulator demonstrated dramatically how a calculating machine could save time, energy, and money in completing a specific task. In the early decades of the new century, punch-card machines were used by the government and private businesses to perform numerous tasks. But the process was complicated, laborious, and limited in its scope. It would take a new device to spur inventors to create the modern computer as we know it today.

THOMAS EDISON (RIGHT) INSPECTS THE VACUUM TUBE HE INVENTED. THE TUBE WAS LATER PUT TO WORK RELAYING ELECTRICAL CURRENT IN COMPUTERS AND OTHER ELECTRONIC DEVICES.

Monster Computers

The vacuum tube had been invented by American Thomas Edison in the 1880s. It resembled an elongated lightbulb with a metal strip or filament inside. The filament, when most of the air was pumped out of the tube (hence its name), worked as a resistor to an electric current, regulating its flow. A series of vacuum tubes created electronic signals or currents and then controlled their output in order to power machinery. Radios were one of the first electronic devices to successfully integrate vacuum tubes.

By the late 1920s, vacuum tubes had begun to replace punch cards in computing machines. Like the cards, the tubes acted as relays, sending information and commands to the machine. Because vacuum tubes were powered by electricity, they worked much faster and more accurately than the cards.

Throughout the 1930s, however, computing machines without vacuum tubes continued to be produced. The differential analyzer was developed by American engineer Vannevar Bush in 1931. The differential analyzer could perform complicated mathematical equations and was the first useful analog computer, a device that uses measurable quantities, such as weight or speed, to represent data rather than numbers.

Five years later, British mathematician Alan Turing proposed in a scientific paper a more ambitious computer that he called the Turing machine. Turing conceived of it as an automatic typewriter that used symbols for mathematical problems instead of letters, making it, in Turing's word, "universal." The Turing machine, although never built, was the ancestor of today's digital computers, based on the binary system.

Birth of the Mark I

The first computing machine to successfully run on vacuum tubes was made by John Vincent Atanasoff and Clifford Berry in 1939 at Iowa State College.

While Atanasoff and Berry were devising their computing machine, Howard Aiken, a graduate student in physics at Harvard University in Massachusetts, was looking for an easier way to get through the seemingly endless calculations he needed to perform in order to complete his doctoral dissertation. In 1937 Aiken thought he had the answer—an automatic calculator made of existing materials. He proposed his Automatic Sequence Controlled Calculator (ASCC) to IBM after being rejected by another company. IBM agreed to build the ASCC, more popularly known as the Mark I, at its laboratories in Endicott, New York. The computer, constructed under the direction of Clair D. Lake, Francis E. Hamilton, and Benjamin M. Durfee, took four years to complete.

The Mark I was unlike any computing machine previously made. Instead of one central computer, it consisted of a complex of 78 separate units, linked by 530 miles (853 kilometers) of wire and containing 2,204 adding wheels and 3,304 electromechanical relays. In total, it was comprised of more than 800,000 separate parts. The enormous machine was 51 feet long (15.5 meters) and 8 feet (2.4 meters) high and weighed 5 tons (4.5 metric tons). A user would program instructions for the computer on a continuous roll of hole-punched paper tape that would then be fed into the machine and direct its actions. Once the paper was inserted, the Mark I worked automatically, without any further human intervention needed, until the calculations were completed. When operating, with its 1,400 rotary switches opening and closing, the Mark I sounded like a noisy array of knitting needles all working at once. Final results from the computer were printed out on IBM typewriters.

THE MARK I, THE FIRST OF THE SUPERSIZED COMPUTERS OF THE 1940S, WAS ALSO THE
FIRST COMPUTER TO "GO TO WAR." IT WAS USED BY THE U.S. NAVY DURING WORLD WAR
II TO CALCULATE THE TRAJECTORY OF ARTILLERY SHELLS.

After successful tests, the Mark I was disassembled and rebuilt at the Research Laboratory of Physics at Harvard University and dedicated on August 7, 1944.

At first, the Mark I must have seemed to many just a curiosity with little practical use outside the halls of academia and science. But that changed quickly when the U.S. Navy took an interest in it. World War II was still raging, and the Navy needed to be able to quickly calculate the trajectory of artillery shells fired from its guns at enemy targets. Aiken leased the Mark I to the U.S. Navy Bureau of Ships for the remainder of the war. The first computing machine used for a military operation, it operated twenty-four hours a day. Aiken went on to develop the Mark II, starting in 1945.

Faster Than Thought

The Mark I was well suited to the specific calculations the navy needed to perform. Its focus was narrow—the calculating of complex mathematical equations. But more and more scientists were looking to create a computer that could both do math problems and process more general information. Such a general-purpose computer could have many practical applications and be utilized in the business world as well as for scientific pursuits.

In 1946, after three years of work, engineer John Presper Eckert and physicist John W. Mauchly completed the first programmable general-purpose electronic computer, at the University of Pennsylvania in Philadelphia. They called it the Electronic Numerical Integrator and Calculator (ENIAC).

If Mark I was a giant, then ENIAC was the true colossus of computers. It took up 1,500 square feet (139 square meters) of space, boasted more than 18,000 vacuum tubes, and weighed more than 30 tons (27 metric tons), six times the weight of the Mark I. The speed with which ENIAC could calculate far eclipsed the rates of other computers of the time. It could solve five thousand addition problems and up to five hundred multiplication problems in a second. In one public demonstration,

The First Computer "Bug"

On September 9, 1947, a hot day in late summer, the Mark II was humming along, when it suddenly came to an abrupt halt. The operations crew began the tedious process of searching the computer for problems. Often a burned-out vacuum tube was the culprit, but not this time. The crew found that a moth had flown into the computer and had been crushed inside a relay. The dead insect was removed with a pair of tweezers and carefully taped into a logbook that recorded all computer activity. A witty crew member wrote this notation beside it: "First actual case of bug being found."

The word *bug,* in this context, referred to a mechanical malfunction and had been used by engineers at least as far back as the 1870s. But that day the Mark II crew invented a new term. When Howard Aiken stopped in to see how his computer was working, someone told him they were "debugging" it. The phrase caught on and is still used today to describe the process of detecting and removing defects or errors from a computer program. The logbook containing the first computer "bug" is in the collection of the National Museum of American History in Washington, D.C.

ENIAC multiplied a five-digit number by itself five thousand times in less than half a second. One reporter gushed that this miraculous machine was "faster than thought."

Fresh from their success, Eckert and Mauchly formed their own computer company, which was bought by Remington-Rand in 1950. The following year, Remington-Rand unveiled the two men's newest model, the Universal Automatic Computer (UNIVAC), which had a wider range of applications than ENIAC and was the first computer to be sold commercially. More compact than its predecessor, it had 5,200 vacuum tubes, took up only 350 square feet (10.4 square meters) of floor space, and weighed a mere 14.5 tons (13 metric tons).

The first model of UNIVAC-I was bought by the U.S. Census Bureau to help with its population count. The fifth UNIVAC-I was used by the CBS television network to predict the 1952 presidential election. With a

THE SPRAWLING NATURE AND COMPLEX DESIGN OF EARLY COMPUTERS ARE DRAMATICALLY SEEN IN THIS PHOTOGRAPH OF A MAN WORKING ON ENIAC, THE FIRST GENERAL-PURPOSE COMPUTER, BUILT IN 1946. ENIAC STANDS FOR "ELECTRONIC NUMERICAL INTEGRATOR AND CALCULATOR."

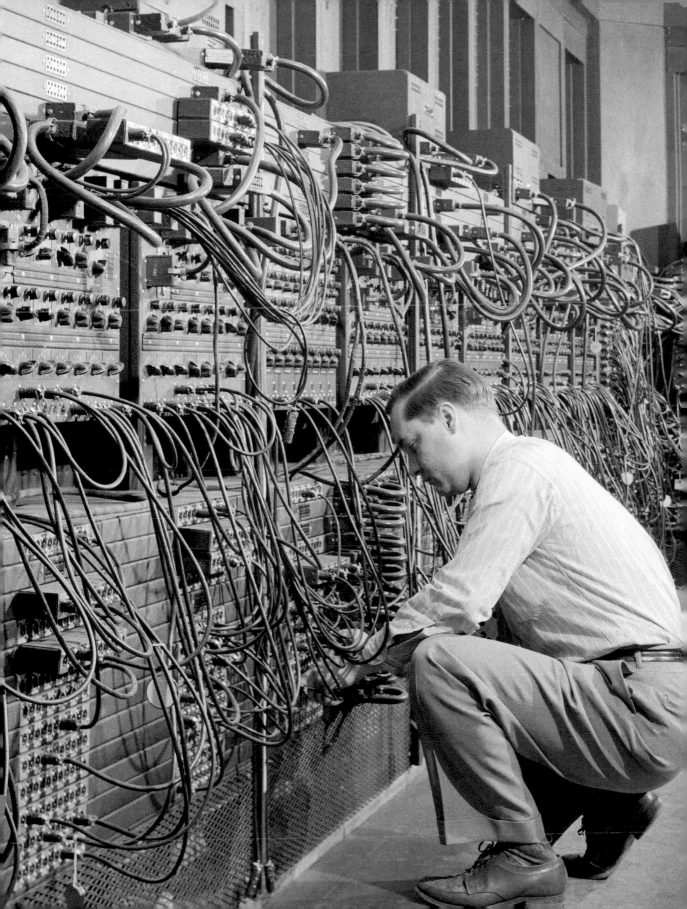

sample of only 1 percent of the voting population, UNIVAC-I correctly predicted that Dwight D. Eisenhower would become the next U.S. president. By 1959 there were 46 UNIVAC-Is across the nation, many of them being used by other government agencies, businesses, and universities.

Problems

Yet for all their accomplishments, these monster computers had one common problem—the vacuum tubes that helped run them. A major drawback was the massive amounts of electricity the tubes used. The UNIVAC, for example, required 150,000 watts of electricity a day. When ENIAC was in operation at night, a nearby town's lights dimmed from the power drain. Vacuum tubes were also only efficient when heated, and the time it took to warm them up was costly. Besides that, they were extremely fragile. The glass could break or air would leak in over time, destroying the vacuum inside the tubes and robbing them of their efficiency. The tubes also burned out regularly. With ENIAC, about two thousand vacuum tubes burned out monthly and had to be replaced by six technicians.

Before computers could advance further, a new means of powering them had to be found.

From Transistors to Microchips

In 1947 Walter Houser Brattain and John Bardeen, two physicists working at Bell Laboratories in Murray Hill, New Jersey, created the first transistor, a tiny device that would create a revolution not just in computers, but in all electronic machines, including radios and television sets.

The transistor was a sophisticated device that used one of the simplest of substances—the element silicon, which is found in rocks and sand. A property of silicon is that it allows electricity to flow through it, but not at a rapid rate. For this reason silicon is called a semiconductor. Brattain and Bardeen used a wafer of germanium, a hard element and semiconductor, as the base for their transistor and pushed a plastic wedge with a strip of gold foil into it. The edges of the foil made contact with the surface, creating a flow of current. By adding certain impurities to the silicon, the flow of electricity through the wafer was improved and at the same time more controllable, making it ideal as a relay or signal in electronic devices. This initial version of the device was called a point-contact transistor.

Solid-state Transistors

Transistors had many advantages over vacuum tubes. Smaller than a penny in size, a transistor was far more compact than a vacuum tube. Computers would no longer have to be gargantuan in size, but could

THESE SILICON WAFERS ARE THE MAIN INGREDIENT IN THE TRANSISTOR, THE DEVICE THAT
REVOLUTIONIZED COMPUTERS AND OTHER ELECTRONIC DEVICES.

become much more streamlined. Transistors were also solid throughout, with none of the empty space found in vacuum tubes, making them sturdier and less likely to break or leak. This led to radios and televisions and later computers being called "solid state." Furthermore, transistors were far less expensive to manufacture and lasted longer than vacuum tubes. But perhaps the greatest advantage was that transistors made machines operate with a far greater speed than before. While vacuum tube computers such as the UNIVAC could perform up to 100,000 addition calculations per second, a so-called "second-generation" transistor computer, such as the IBM 7090, could perform up to 229,000 addition problems per second.

The transition from vacuum tube to transistor-based computers, however, was a slow one that took years to complete. Brattain, Bardeen, and William Shockley, who supervised their research and later made further improvements on transistors, were awarded a Nobel Prize in Physics for their work in 1956. Transistor-run computers did not appear on the market until the following year.

Part of the reason for the delay was the difficulties of applying transistors to machines. The transistors had to be connected to one another by intricate wiring in a series to form larger circuit boards. The boards were, unlike the transistors themselves, big and unwieldy. Furthermore, the fragile wires connecting the transistors could easily break.

Birth of the Microchip

In 1959 two technicians, working independently, came up with the answer to the circuit board problem. Jack Kilby at Texas Instruments worked out a way to combine the electronic transistor with a silicon chip. About the same time, Robert Noyce at Fairchild Semiconductor found a way to carve patterns using acids in a silicon wafer and embed wires in these patterns to connect the transistors. Whereas before the circuit wires and transistors were separate components, now they were joined together in one unit. The result was called an integrated circuit (IC) or more commonly a microchip.

JOHN BARDEEN, WILLIAM SHOCKLEY, AND WALTER BRATTAIN (FROM LEFT TO RIGHT)
SHARED A NOBEL PRIZE FOR PHYSICS IN 1956 FOR THEIR DEVELOPMENT OF THE TRANSISTOR.
BARDEEN AND BRATTAIN ACTUALLY CREATED THE FIRST TRANSISTOR, AND SHOCKLEY LATER
IMPROVED ON IT.

William Shockley—Father of Silicon Valley

A cantankerous and controversial figure, William Shockley was once called by his admirers "the man who brought silicon to Silicon Valley."

He was born in London, England, in 1910 to American parents and raised in California. After receiving his doctoral degree from the Massachusetts Institute of Technology (MIT) in 1936, Shockley joined a top research team at Bell Labs in New Jersey. When his assistants Bardeen and Brattain made their discovery of a point-contact transistor, Shockley tried to take the credit, but failed. He did go on to conduct his own groundbreaking work with transistors and created an improved one-piece junction transistor in 1951 that superseded the less effective point-contact transistor.

Shockley left Bell in 1954 and joined Beckman Instruments, where he was appointed director of the new Shockley Semiconductor Laboratory in Mountain View, California. For four years he continued to work on silicon semiconductors, but in 1957 decided to end that phase of his research. Eight members of his staff, who he branded "the Traitorous Eight," quit in frustration and started their own company, Fairchild Semiconductor Corporation. Among the eight were Robert Noyce, creator of the microchip, and other pioneers of what would come to be called Silicon Valley.

Shockley became a professor of engineering at Stanford University in 1963 and remained there until 1975. In the early 1970s he began his controversial work in human intelligence. Shockley claimed that white people were genetically more intelligent than black people. His theories were then, and now, strenuously discredited by a majority of leading scientists in the field. By the time of his death in 1989, Shockley's reputation had been seriously tarnished by his later work and writings.

By the early 1960s the IC led to a new third generation of computers, smaller, faster and ten times more powerful than the transistor computers that immediately preceded them.

Part of the impetus to shrink the size of computers through smaller ICs was in response to the emerging space race between the Soviet Union and the United States. In 1957 the Soviets sent the first artificial satellite, *Sputnik I,* into space. The United States, for scientific and political reasons, wanted to compete and surpass the Soviet Union in space exploration. To break the bonds of gravity and to soar into space, rockets and other missiles had to be lightweight. Computers thus had to become smaller and more compact to achieve this end. The National Aeronautics and Space Association (NASA) picked Noyce's IC to run the computers in their spacecraft. In 1968 Noyce cofounded an electronics company, Intel. The following year one of his researchers, Ted Hoff, began to design a chip that contained all the components of a computer's central processing unit (CPU), the part of the computer that contains its circuitry. This "computer on a chip" came to be called a microprocessor. Hoff's first microcomputer was only ⅛ by ⅙ inches (0.32 by 0.42 centimeters), but had power and capabilities equal to the enormous ENIAC. The first microprocessor became available commercially in 1971.

While microprocessors were mostly used by commercial and governmental groups, there was at least one invention that used ICs that could benefit the general public—the pocket calculator. The first hand-held calculator was the Sharp EL-8, unveiled in January 1971. It weighed about a pound (0.45 kilograms), had a fluorescent display, was powered by rechargeable batteries, and retailed for about 395 dollars. Texas Instruments came out with the SR-10 (SR stood for "slide rule") in 1973. It was able to add, subtract, multiply, divide, and do algebraic problems. Suddenly the slide rule and logarithm tables had become obsolete. Hewlett Packard's HP-65 of 1974 then emerged as the powerhouse of pocket calculators. The HP-65 had a capacity of one hundred instructions and could store and retrieve programs, using a built-in

ROBERT NOYCE POSES FOR A *TIME* MAGAZINE PHOTOGRAPHER WITH THE INTEGRATED CIRCUIT THAT HE HELPED PIONEER AT HIS COMPANY INTEL IN THE LATE 1960S.

A SMILING JACK KILBY IS SURROUNDED BY ELECTRONIC DEVICES PRODUCED BY TEXAS INSTRUMENTS, THE COMPANY HE WORKED FOR WHEN HE COINVENTED THE INTEGRATED

CIRCUIT. HE WAS AWARDED A NOBEL PRIZE FOR PHYSICS IN 2000 FOR HIS DISCOVERY.

An Wang

Nearly as important to the development of computer technology as the invention of the transistor was the invention of the magnetic pulse transfer controlling device. It allowed computer-stored magnetic memory to be read without being destroyed in the process.

The man who coinvented this device was Chinese American An Wang. Wang—who was born in Shanghai, China, in 1920—immigrated to the United States at the age of twenty-five to attend Harvard University. He graduated with a PhD in applied physics in 1948 after working with Howard Aiken on the Mark IV, Aiken's first fully electronic computer. It was during this time that Wang invented the pulse transfer controlling device, which spurred the development of magnetic core computer memory.

He founded Wang Laboratories in 1951, which manufactured electronic calculators and, later, word processors and computers. Although the company's early years were difficult ones, by 1964 sales had reached one million dollars. The Wang Loci-2, unveiled in 1965, was most likely the first desktop computer that could compute logarithms. The company then developed the Wang 2200 in 1976, one of the first desktop computers with a large cathode-ray tube (CRT) display.

Wang was a great benefactor of his adopted state of Massachusetts, where his company was located. He helped restore Boston's Metropolitan Theatre, which was renamed the Wang Theatre in 1983. Boston is also home to the Wang Center for the Performing Arts. An Wang died of cancer in 1990.

magnetic card reader. Texas Instruments' TI-30, which debuted in 1985, became one of the biggest-selling pocket calculators of all time.

While calculators had been around for decades, the new pocket calculator was something new. It could perform an amazing number of functions with just the press of a button. Some computer scientists began to consider if a calculator could be made to meet the needs of the average person, why not a computer?

THE ALTAIR 8800, THE WORLD'S FIRST HOME COMPUTER, IS POSITIVELY PRIMITIVE WHEN COMPARED TO THE PCs OF TODAY.

Computers Get Personal

The idea of a personal computer or PC for the home, which the average person could use for various tasks, was not a notion that many took seriously in the early 1970s. Experts believed that computers, whatever their size and capabilities, were meant for large companies, scientific organizations, and government agencies, not for the family den or home office.

However, the phenomenal success of the pocket calculator prompted some manufacturers to think there might be a market for a small, personal computer that could be used in the home or office. They were also encouraged by the growing number of enthusiasts and hobbyists both in the computer field and outside it.

The Altair 8800

In 1975 the small company Micro Instrumentation and Telemetry Systems (MITS) unveiled the world's first home computer, the Altair 8800. It bore little resemblance to the sophisticated personal computers we know today. For one thing, the Altair 8800 was sold as a "kit" to be assembled by the purchaser. It had no monitor, no keyboard, no disk drive to input data or software program to direct the computer's operation. The owner was required to create his or her own programs in a binary code. To do this, the user flicked switches on the computer's front panel to create each binary digit. The Altair's random access memory

(RAM)—its memory storage used for creating, loading, and running programs—was a mere 256 bytes. That was about enough to store a paragraph of text. The price for this extremely limited computing machine was 395 dollars.

Despite its limitations, the Altair 8800 seized the imagination of computer buffs and hobbyists, who shared their enthusiasm with others via computer clubs, newsletters, and conventions.

One of these early computer enthusiasts was Bill Gates, a young Harvard student majoring in prelaw. When he first read about the Altair 8800 in an issue of *Popular Electronics,* Gates contacted MITS and told company officials that he could create an operating language for their new computer. He was convincing, and MITS expressed interest. Gates, with his friend Paul Allen, created a BASIC (Beginner's All-purpose Symbolic Instruction Code) program for the Altair in just eight weeks, beating out other competitors for the job. MITS bought the program, and in 1975 Gates dropped out of Harvard and started his own software company with Allen. They called it Micro-Soft.

The next enterprising company to enter the home computer market was Atari, the video game company, which had pioneered video games in the early 1970s using computer technology. The Atari 400 looked like a glorified typewriter that used a television screen as a monitor for displaying prerecorded computer programs played on a special tape deck.

Like the Altair 8800, the Atari 400 was extremely limited, but its successor, the Atari 800, was enhanced by colorful graphics and good sound. Its eight thousand bytes of RAM were an enormous improvement over earlier PCs.

The Birth of Apple

Among the young technicians who worked at Atari in 1974 was Steve Jobs, a college dropout from Los Altos, California. Jobs's friend and fellow computer whiz Steve Wozniak designed his own personal computer in 1976, and Jobs persuaded Wozniak to start a company to market his computer. They filed the papers incorporating their Apple Computer

BILL GATES DEVELOPED AND SOLD THE SOFTWARE PROGRAM WINDOWS 1.0 THROUGH HIS CORPORATION, MICROSOFT. IT WOULD FAIL, BUT WINDOWS 3.0 WOULD BE A STUNNING SUCCESS.

company on April 1, 1976. The date, April Fool's Day, was significant, for both young men had a keen sense of humor. For example, they priced their first computer, the Apple I, at $666.66, which duplicated digits from "Woz's" Dial-a-Joke telephone number. Sales of Apple I were modest, but the Apple II, released in 1977, was an instant hit with consumers.

The Apple II looked like a portable appliance with its beige plastic case and keyboard. It was advertised as the first "complete, ready-to-use personal computer." Although it had no monitor, when hooked up to a television screen the Apple II offered high-resolution graphics, excellent sound, and built-in BASIC programming that was easy to master. The Apple II was the first personal computer that could be used by anyone—home owners, small business owners, and students. It gradually became the standard computer in the elementary and high school classroom where it proved an excellent learning tool when loaded with interactive educational software.

The Apple II Plus boasted its own monitor and two disk drives through which software could be installed. It was the first personal computer with its own floppy disk drive. Floppy disks are used to store computer data and programs. But not all of Apple's computers were successes. The Apple III, the company's first PC aimed for business use, came out in 1980 was a failure. It was too expensive for the marketplace (3,495 dollars) and was plagued by bugs in its system that took time to eliminate. The Apple Lisa (Local Integrated Software Architecture), released in 1983, was the company's most powerful personal computer, with a graphical user interface and a mouse, a device used to select items onscreen. The Lisa was aimed largely at the business market. Again, its cost was too high—9,995 dollars—and it quickly failed.

The Microsoft Revolution

The success of the Apple II convinced the computer giant IBM to get into the PC market. In 1980 IBM began to build the frame and the mechanical and electronic components, called the hardware, for its first

THE FREEWHEELING STYLE OF THE FOUNDERS OF APPLE COMPUTERS IS CAPTURED IN THIS PHOTOGRAPH OF COFOUNDER STEVE WOZNIAK HUGGING HIS MACINTOSH LAPTOP POWERBOOK WHILE LEADING A CONGA LINE OF EQUALLY ENTHUSIASTIC SCHOOLCHILDREN EQUIPPED WITH THEIR OWN MODELS AS WELL.

"desktop" computer, but the company lacked the expertise to create the software-based operating system (OS) needed to make it function.

They turned to Bill Gates's fledgling Microsoft company. Gates referred IBM to Digital Research, a company in Monterey, California, that he thought could handle the job better than he could. But when Digital Research did not respond to IBM's calls, they returned to Gates, who agreed to give it a try.

Bill Gates

The richest man in the world in 2006, Bill Gates built his computer software empire on his programming skills and business savvy. He was born in 1955 in Seattle, Washington, into an affluent family. His father was a leading attorney and his mother a civic leader. Gates was a top student in math and science and founded a company while still in high school that sold traffic flow data to state governments. He attended Harvard but dropped out after his second year to found Microsoft, a software company.

Microsoft's phenomenal success came as much from Gates's business acumen as from his technological expertise. He got IBM to preinstall DOS on their PCs, giving him a monopoly in the market. He also earned millions licensing the software to other companies as MS-DOS (Microsoft Disk Operating System).

In 2000 Gates and his wife founded the Bill and Melinda Gates Foundation, a charitable organization that donates funds to a host of causes from college scholarships for needy minority students to AIDS prevention. As of 2006 the foundation had an endowment of $31.9 billion. On June 15 of that year, Gates announced that by mid-2008 he would make the transition from overseeing the day-to-day operations of Microsoft to devote most of his time and energies to his foundation.

Gates bought the rights to QDOS (Quick and Dirty Operating System) from Seattle Computer Products for 56,000 dollars, and IBM used it in its computer, renaming it PC-DOS. The IBM PC went on the market in 1981 and sold 100,000 units in its first year. The following year people bought 2.5 million personal computers, and the PC was named *Time* magazine's Machine of the Year. Many who could afford it wanted a PC for their home. They used their PCs as word processors to write letters, collect recipes, and keep track of personal finances, bills, addresses, and daily chores.

Apple versus IBM

After several years of missteps and disappointments, Apple was back on top of the PC market with the Apple MacIntosh, introduced in 1984. It

THE PERSONAL COMPUTER HAD TRULY ARRIVED WHEN *TIME* MAGAZINE NAMED IT THE
MACHINE OF THE YEAR IN 1982.

was far more user-friendly than IBM PCs and the growing number of IBM clones put out by other manufacturers. Users could perform functions by clicking on colorful graphic elements or icons, a much simpler process than inputting the complicated computer commands that DOS demanded. With its great range of font sizes and design options, Macintosh helped give birth to desktop publishing, allowing users to create their own newsletters, greeting cards, and many other kinds of printed material. Macintosh quickly surpassed IBM's PCs in the marketplace.

Bill Gates rose to the challenge, and Microsoft developed its own version of a graphical user interface (GUI), replacing commands with icons. By the mid-1980s, the first Microsoft "Windows" software was released by Microsoft for use by IBM as an alternative to its DOS software and as a direct competitor with Macintosh.

While early versions of Windows had many bugs that needed to be worked out, Windows 3.0, released in 1990, proved effective and efficient. It sold ten million copies in just two years. Windows made the IBM PCs dominant in the home computer market, and made Microsoft Incorporated the leading software company in the world.

Steve Jobs and NeXT

While Microsoft and IBM were solidifying a successful partnership, Apple was experiencing serious internal turmoil. At the center of the storm was Steve Jobs—a visionary who could also be extremely difficult to work with. Jobs left Apple in 1985, although he remained chairman of Apple Computer. He founded a new company, NeXT Computers Incorporated.

NeXT's focus was not the general home computer market, but the leading edge of new computer technology. While many of its computer models were too expensive to sell widely, they incorporated such important innovations as the Session Description Protocol (SDP) charge, a format for describing streaming media or media viewed as it is being received, and a built-in port for Ethernet, a computer technology for local area networks.

STEVE JOBS, COFOUNDER OF APPLE, POSES WITH THE APPLE II COMPUTER. JOBS WOULD LEAVE APPLE IN 1985 AND ESTABLISH NEXT COMPUTERS INCORPORATED, A COMPANY HE PUT ON THE CUTTING EDGE OF COMPUTER TECHNOLOGY.

In 1990 Jobs launched his NeXTcube, a complex PC that he described as an "interpersonal" computer, taking the home computer to the next logical step of development. The goal in creating and marketing NeXTcube was to allow home and business computers to link to other computers in order to communicate and share information. While this concept had been recognized and pursued for several decades, it would only come to full fruition in the 1990s, producing a major revolution in the way people around the world communicate and receive information.

The Information Highway

The idea of a network of computers that could share and exchange data began as a defensive action during the cold war between the United States and the Soviet Union. It would eventually lead to an interconnected world and help pave the way for the burgeoning global economy to come.

The Evolution of the Internet

In 1958 the U.S. Department of Defense formed the Advanced Research Projects Agency (ARPA). Its purpose was to set up a computer-networking system that could function even if key government computers were destroyed in a Soviet attack. In 1962 ARPA began a research project to link networks of computers and develop common rules or protocols that could allow these linked networks to communicate with one another. "I was interested in a new way of doing things," said Dr. J.C.R. Licklider, who was put in charge of the project. After seven years of work, Licklider's team of computer scientists completed ARPANET, the world's first computer network. ARPANET connected computer networks from nodes at four universities in California and Utah. By 1971 twenty-three universities, corporations, and government research centers were linked by ARPANET and able to communicate with one another through electronic mail or text messaging via computer, later commonly called e-mail.

THE INTERNET, AN INDISPENSABLE PART OF MODERN COMMUNICATIONS, HAS BEEN EVOLVING SINCE AT LEAST THE EARLY 1970S.

Telenet, a commercial version of ARPANET developed for use by the general public, was established in 1974, but initial interest was limited. The average person found Telenet a difficult-to-access and cumbersome tool that they had little use for.

One thing the network lacked was a common language that users of different kinds and brands of computers and those in foreign countries could use to communicate with one another. In 1978 after several years of work, computer scientists Vinton Cerf and Robert Kahn designed a

MAKING THE INTERNET ACCESSIBLE TO THE AVERAGE COMPUTER USER, THROUGH EFFECTIVE COMMANDS AND PROTOCOLS, WAS LARGELY THE WORK OF VINTON CERF (LEFT) AND ROBERT KAHN, WHO HAVE BEEN DUBBED TWO OF THE "FOUNDING FATHERS OF THE INTERNET."

coded language called Transmission Control Protocol/Internet Protocol (TCP/IP) that standardized communications by 1982. More accessible than before, the network link-up drew in a growing number of college students and businesspeople. It became known as simply the Internet.

The Creation of the World Wide Web

To make the Internet attractive to more people, it needed programs and tools that would make it even easier to access and use. It would also have to have something to offer its users in terms of informational value. Tim Berners-Lee, an English computer programmer working at the European Center for Nuclear Research known as CERN near Geneva, Switzerland, thought he had the solution. "I happened to come along . . . after hypertext [written text on the computer screen] and the Internet had come of age. The task left to me was to marry them together," wrote Berners-Lee. Hypertext is a very different kind of script from the text in a book, magazine, or newspaper. It contains hyperlinks, words or pictures highlighted or underlined in the text. When clicked on with a cursor, a tool indicating where data may be input on a computer screen, the user would be transferred to a new text or Web page that provided him or her with different information. These interlinks were all connected to the original topic being investigated or researched, a network of linked information that Berners-Lee likened to a web with many strands that all were connected to one another. Therefore a hypertext document on a computer screen became a Web page, and a collection of pages that formed a unit became a Web site with its own computer address or uniform resource locator (URL). The home page was the first page that came into view on a Web site. The end of the URL told the user that the owner of the Web site was a government agency (gov), part of the military (mil), a privately owned company (com), a nonprofit organization (org), or a college or university (edu).

In 1990 Berners-Lee began to work on an Internet-based system for sharing information. His ultimate goal was to expand the system, making it global in scope—the World Wide Web (WWW). Working closely

TIM BERNERS-LEE, AN ENGLISH COMPUTER PROGRAMMER, INVENTED THE WORLD WIDE WEB IN 1990 AND HAS BEEN WATCHING OVER IT EVER SINCE. HE IS NOW WORKING ON A NEW PROJECT, THE SEMANTIC WEB, THAT WILL ATTEMPT TO ORGANIZE DATA MORE EFFECTIVELY.

with Belgian engineer Robert Cailliau, an experienced CERN manager, Berners-Lee worked with a NeXT computer's operating system to create his own system. He tried to implement a Web browser, a computer program that would allow him to open and display hypertext documents, but the software companies he enlisted in his search could not understand how such a system could function without a central manager or database. Berners-Lee explained that his system had to be open-ended and allow users to access information without the burden of dealing directly with individual servers. Without outside help, Berners-Lee was forced to rely on his own skills and imagination.

He developed a set of procedures that would call up hypertext documents on the Internet on request. He called it hypertext transfer protocol (HTTP). It would enable a host computer to link a requested file on its internal hard drive and transmit it to the computer of the person who requested it. On arrival, the HTML (Hypertext Markup Language) would display the document as a Web page.

Berners-Lee had all the components for his World Wide Web. He then created software on which to store the hypertext files and loaded them onto a high-speed computer connected to the Internet.

Before the end of 1990, his system was up and running with the world's first Web page. Surprisingly, few people at CERN recognized the significance of the Web. But researchers at other companies were more impressed. Berners-Lee released his Web browser, a software program to load and display Web pages, and server on the Internet to be downloaded by anyone anywhere with a computer. In 1992 there were 1,000 hits or user visits to the CERN server. A year later, that number climbed to 10,000.

The World Wide Web was becoming a kind of global club, where users contacted Berners-Lee to praise him and offer constructive criticism on how he could make his product better. He listened carefully and used these suggestions to improve and refine the components of the World Wide Web.

Marc Andreessen and the First Web Browser

One of the central reasons why Web users grew tenfold in 1993 was the emergence of the first easy-to-use browser to navigate the World Wide Web. Browsers, such of Berners-Lee's, were available, but did not display images and text together. Any graphic elements could be viewed only in separate files. In late 1992 Marc Andreessen and Eric Bina, working at the National Center for Supercomputing Applications (NCSA) at the University of Illinois at Urbana-Champaign, set out to create a user-friendly program that would wed images and text on the same Web page. They completed their browser, Mosaic, six months later, and made it free to all users. Within a year, more than two million copies of Mosaic were downloaded on the Internet.

In 1994 Andreessen and software executive Jim Clark founded Netscape Communications—which featured a commercial browser, Navigator—that they offered free to users. In one year, more than eight million copies of Navigator were downloaded. Netscape made its income from selling software to companies wanting to create their own Web sites. Navigator remained the dominant Web browser until Microsoft unveiled its own browser, Internet Explorer, in 1995.

The WWW Consortium

By the mid-1990s, the World Wide Web was being used by more and more people around the world. As usage increased, there was a growing need for better controls and rules on the Web. One of Berners-Lee's fears was that rival company browsers would fragment the Web into smaller networks that would not be easily accessible to everyone.

In 1994 he helped create the World Wide Web Consortium (W3C), a supervisory organization composed of members representing the great variety of companies and agencies doing business on the Web and concerned for its future. The consortium originally had two headquarters—at the Massachusetts Institute of Technology (MIT), supervised by Berners-Lee, and at CERN in Switzerland, which was soon replaced

GOOGLE, THE MOST POPULAR AND BEST KNOWN INTERNET SEARCH ENGINE, WAS THE BRAIN-CHILD OF LARRY PAGE (LEFT) AND SERGEY BRIN, WHO FOUNDED THE COMPANY IN 1998.

by the National Institute for Research in Computer Science and Language in France. In 2003 the National Institute was replaced by the European Research Consortium in Informatics and Mathematics. An Asian headquarters was added in 1996 at Keio University in Japan. As of 2006 the W3C had more than four hundred members. It discusses problems on the Web, such as hacking or illegal break-ins and other related issues of security. The W3C also works out new protocols to be used on the WWW to improve it.

Building a Better Search Engine

As more and more sites appeared on the World Wide Web, it became a veritable information highway that could take the user to any field of learning or expertise that he or she desired. But navigating this highway could be difficult and time consuming. Although browsers such as Netscape Navigator and Microsoft's Internet Explorer allowed easy access to the Internet and its wonders, they did not always point users in the direction of the information they wanted. If the searcher did not have the exact URL address of a Web site, how would he or she find it? Companies began to design search engines, software programs that allowed users to search for Web pages by entering specific keywords.

Google, the most pervasive search engine on the Web today, began as a research project of Larry Page and Sergey Brin, two PhD students at Stanford University in California. Most search engines up to that time ranked their results of a search according to the number of times the keyword appeared on a page. This led to a large number of "misfits," when the word was interpreted incorrectly and turned up the wrong Web sites. Page and Brin decided to base their search engine on an analysis of the relationships among Web pages in order to improve accuracy in the search.

On September 15, 1997, the two officially registered the domain name google.com and formally incorporated about a year later, using a friend's garage in Menlo Park, California, as their corporate headquarters. Google is a misspelling of the word googol, a mathematical term for

Wikipedia—the Web's Ever-growing Encyclopedia

One of the most useful and ambitious Web sites is Wikipedia, an online encyclopedia. This enormous compendium of universal knowledge was cocreated in January 2001 by Jimmy Wales, a former options trader. Wales started it as a complement to another Web encyclopedia, Nupedia, developed, like most traditional encyclopedias, by a staff of experts in various fields. Wales envisioned Wikipedia as something quite different. *Wiki-Wiki* is Hawaiian for "hurry quick," and Wiki in computer terminology has come to mean "a Web site that allows users to edit its content to make it more accurate and up-to-date." To assure accuracy and fairness, Wikipedia has an army of "core regulars" who constantly check all changes to its content. As inaccuracies emerged in Wikipedia's content, contributors were required to register before creating new pages.

JIMMY WALES HELPED BUILD HIS WIKIPEDIA SITE INTO THE VAST INFORMATION RESOURCE IT IS TODAY. HE REMAINS DEDICATED TO BRINGING WIKI-BASED PROJECTS TO THE COMPUTING COMMUNITY FREE OF COST.

Eventually Wikipedia completely eclipsed Nupedia and the original English-language version was joined by Wikipedias in other languages, including German, France, Chinese, Dutch, Russian, and even the international language of Esperanto. On March 1, 2006, the English-language Wikipedia posted its one millionth article. The site has truly fulfilled Wales goal of becoming "the largest encyclopedia ever written."

the number one followed by one hundred zeros. Page and Brin aspired with their search engine to organize and make accessible to computer users a seemingly infinite amount of data on the Web. Google quickly attracted users with its simple yet attractive design, uncluttered by advertisements. When the company eventually included ads starting in 2000, they wisely filtered in only those ads that were directly associated with the person's keyword search.

By early 2004 Google was handling about 85 percent of all search requests on the World Wide Web. In September 2005 the company expanded its horizons by entering into a partnership with the National Aeronautics and Space Administration (NASA) to work on data management. Today the verb *google,* meaning "to use Google to perform a Web search," is a part of standard English.

E-mail, Chat Rooms, and Blogs

The information highway soon proved to be a two-way street. Users could access information, but they could also reach out to communicate to others, have open discussions on any topic that interested them, and even express their own opinions and thoughts to anyone with access to the Internet.

Electronic mail, better known as e-mail, began in 1965, predating the Internet by two and a half decades. At first it allowed users to communicate through text messages with others connected to the same mainframe who used it at different times. Within a year, e-mail capability spread to a network of computers, allowing users of different computers on the same network to send messages back and forth to one another.

While ARPANET was pioneering e-mail by 1971, it was not until the 1980s that another network, the Internet Engineering Task Force (IETF), came up with a clear and simple conveyance system—the Simple Mail Transfer Protocol (SMTP) that is still used today to transmit e-mail. This procedure relays text messages to a central server, which then sends each message on to the specified recipient. The message

THE LAPTOP COMPUTER, FIRST DEVELOPED IN 1981, DID NOT BECOME PRACTICAL UNTIL THE 1990S.

goes into a message or mail box and can be accessed and read at any time by the recipient who can then respond to it.

Once limited to a few users on the same computer, today e-mail is used by millions of PC or Macintosh users for both business and personal correspondence. Checking your e-mail is a task most PC users do daily, if not more frequently. The proliferation of e-mail was initially a serious threat to the regular postal service (called snail mail by many people because of its relative slowness). But more recently, the postal service has benefited from e-mail as the owners and users of such major sites as Amazon.com and eBay, an auction site, use the postal service for mailing millions of packages to online purchasers.

Of course, like the postal service, e-mail has its share of junk mail, known as spam. Spam is so cheap to send electronically that companies, called spammers, often send out millions of unsolicited messages daily promoting products and services to PC users. This proliferation of spam has become a major annoyance, often clogging up e-mail mailboxes and even preventing users from receiving more meaningful correspondence. In 2003 the U.S. Congress passed the Can Spam Act to regulate and cut down on spam e-mail.

While e-mail allows users to communicate one-on-one through text messaging, chat rooms allow any number of users to meet on the Internet to talk and discuss common interests in real time. One of the first and most popular of these sites was the Internet Relay Chat (IRC) site, launched in 1988. IRC and other early chat room sites from the 1990s were exclusively text based, but more recent chat rooms have visual and audio capabilities. Users can view a two-dimensional graphic (such as a photograph) of one another as they talk or even hear the person's actual voice speaking to them. Three-dimensional chat rooms in which users can share videos of themselves in their home environment are a more recent development.

Not surprisingly, many chat rooms are aimed at people who are seeking romantic mates. Others are devoted to discussions of politics, movies, and a myriad of other subjects.

Another form of reaching out to others online is the weblog, short-ened to blog, a site where users can write their own diaries or journals that can be viewed by anyone with access to the Internet. The first blogs began to appear in 1994 and were written mostly by college stu-dents. Open Diary, launched in 1998, became the first blog site which allowed readers to respond to and comment on a blogger's entries.

Many people initially viewed blogs as self-indulgent and rather triv-ial. That attitude changed in 2002, when bloggers broke a major news story that had been largely overlooked by the traditional media. They publicized allegedly racist remarks made on the floor of the U.S. Senate by Minority Leader Trent Lott praising retiring senator Strom Thur-mond. Thurmond had run for president in 1948 on the segregationist "Dixiecrat" third-party ticket. The controversy caused Lott to step down as minority leader.

With this display of blogging's increasing popularity and influence, it suddenly became a legitimate form of news media, and by 2004 blogs were being used by political candidates and news services to dissemi-nate information and gather consensus. Former Vermont governor Howard Dean used the Internet and blogs extensively in his unsuccess-ful bid for the Democratic presidential nomination in 2004. The prolif-eration of blogs in recent years has been staggering. Xanga, one of the first blog sites online, had only one hundred diaries registered in 1997. As of December 2005 that number had grown to more than fifty million.

SIX

Computers Today

Today computers play a part in nearly every aspect of our lives. They help us to learn, to work, to communicate with others, and are a source of entertainment and recreation. Larger, more powerful so-called supercomputers are used in the sciences, industry, and education to track weather patterns, improve methods of space travel, teach complicated subjects, and create incredibly lifelike animated films with three-dimensional characters.

Recent advances in computer technology have improved the flow of communications and knowledge and greatly enriched our lives. But innovation often comes at a price. New problems, some of them unique to the computer age, have posed challenges that our society continues to struggle with.

Supercomputers at Work

Supercomputers now play a significant role in nearly every branch of science, used to collect and interpret data. Meteorologists enlist the aid of computers to study world weather patterns and simulate weather phenomenon, such as hurricanes, in order to better understand and respond to them. Biologists use supercomputers to study and evaluate agricultural pests and the ways to best control them. Astronomers use computers to study such phenomenon as black holes and synthesize data on the origins of the universe. Geneticists working on the Human

THE IMAGINED REALM THIS GIRL IS VIEWING THROUGH A VIRTUAL-REALITY SIMULATOR SO POWERFULLY RESEMBLES THE ACTUAL WORLD THAT SHE TRIES TO REACH OUT AND TOUCH IT.

Genome Project (HGP), launched in 1990, have found computers indispensable in mapping and determining the sequence of the three billion nucleotides in the human genome. The data was completed in April 2003 and will be used to find new ways to detect a predisposition for breast cancer and other diseases and possibly to treat genetic-based diseases such as early-onset Alzheimer's disease and certain cancers.

Virtual Reality

One of the greatest accomplishments in computer technology is the creation of virtual reality (VR). VR is the simulation of a three-dimensional environment that appears real to the person viewing it. Computers create virtual reality with sensors, components that detect the viewer's reaction or movements, and effectors that work to stimulate the viewer's senses. Computer hardware links the sensors and effectors to complete the illusion of virtual reality. Another component may be a head-mounted display worn by the person to view the artificial environment. Most VR experiences are primarily visual, but more recently some have included sound and tactile sensations.

What are the practical applications of this astonishing technology? VR can help train surgeons in operational techniques or train astronauts for space flight and the conditions they will encounter on other planets. It can also be used to train soldiers for combat situations and help scientists explore and better understand unique environments too dangerous to enter physically, such as the interior of an active volcano.

The ultimate goal of many scientists who utilize virtual reality is to completely immerse the person in the re-created environment. In April 2005 Sony announced that it had received a patent for the noninvasive beaming of frequencies and ultrasonic waves directly into the human brain to simulate all five senses, including smell and taste.

Computer Animation

Related to virtual reality technology is computer animation, the creation of images using computers. Like virtual reality, computer animation

Deep Blue—the Computer that Mastered Chess

What are the limits of what a computer can do? Student Feng-hsuing Hsu might have asked himself that question when he developed a chess-playing computer called Chiptest in 1985 at Carnegie Mellon University in Pittsburgh, Pennsylvania. Over the next decade, Hsu and others, with the support of IBM, developed the computer, renamed Deep Blue, a derivation of IBM's nickname Big Blue. It had a processor chip specially designed for chess strategy, capable of examining and evaluating up to two hundred million chessboard positions per second.

In February 1996 IBM challenged world chess master Garry Kasparov of the Soviet Union to play against Deep Blue. Kasparov won three out of six games. The computer was further refined, and a second tournament was set for March 1997. This time the computer beat Kasparov 2-1, with three games ending in a draw. Kasparov declined to play Deep Blue again.

While the computer's victory was significant, it was only the start of what scientists think computers can achieve as problem solvers in the future. Today parts of Deep Blue are on display at both the Smithsonian's National Museum of American History in Washington, D.C., and the Computer History Museum in Mountain View, California.

CHESS MASTER GARRY KASPAROV BEAT DEEP BLUE, THE CHESS-PLAYING COMPUTER, IN
THEIR FIRST SHOWDOWN IN 1996, BUT LOST TO THE MACHINE AT THEIR SECOND MEETING
THE FOLLOWING YEAR.

LAPTOPS CAN BE USED ALMOST ANYWHERE, ONE REASON FOR THEIR GREAT POPULARITY.

piece by piece on a computer monitor starting with the skeleton. Then the animation is rendered, using more frames than traditional hand-drawn animation. The result is smoother physical movements, making the characters more realistic. *Toy Story,* the first full-length film made completely by computer animation, was released by Walt Disney Pictures in 1995. While most computer animation films since then have concentrated on cartoonlike characters, the 2001 film *Final Fantasy: The Spirits Within* depicted realistic-looking human characters for the first time. There may come a day when live actors are no longer needed, except to provide voices, in films that are completely computerized.

A Computer in Your Lap

While large computer networks have transformed science and industry, the more visible and perhaps impactful aspect of the computer revolution can be witnessed in the home and beyond. Personal computers are growing smaller and smaller to meet the needs of the general public. By the early 1980s, scientists were working to design a completely portable personal computer that was small enough for the user to carry wherever he or she went. The first portable computer to be sold commercially was the Osborne 1, unveiled in 1981. A breakthrough, it was not without its limitations. The Osborne 1 was about the size of a sewing machine, was heavy, and needed an external power source to operate. While better battery-operated models appeared over the next few years, they were too expensive for most people's budgets. The GRID Compass 1101, for example, retailed at nearly ten thousand dollars.

The first true success in laptop computers was the Apple PowerBook, which debuted in 1991. It was the first of its kind to feature an authentic touchpad, a trackball for a pointing device, and a built-in Ethernet network adapter for connecting to the Internet. Through the 1990s laptops because cheaper and more popular not just with businesspeople on the go, but other professionals, college students, and just about everyone else.

Going to work with
an Osborne
Personal Business
Computer.

OSBORNE
COMPUTER CORPORATION

THE OSBORNE I, RELEASED IN 1981, WAS THE FIRST PORTABLE COMPUTER SOLD
COMMERCIALLY. ALTHOUGH THIS ADVERTISEMENT ATTEMPTS TO PITCH THE PRODUCT TO
BUSINESSPEOPLE ON THE GO, THE MACHINE WAS CUMBERSOME AND EXPENSIVE.

Laptops are so useful that one American university is trying to make them available for global education. The Massachusetts Institute of Technology's Media Lab's One Laptop Per Child project is working to design, make, and distribute the computers to every child in the world.

In the Palm of Your Hand

While there are now personal computers that can fit in your lap, there are also wireless communication devices that can fit in your hand. While not true computers, they contain microprocessors and can perform many of the same functions that personal computers do.

The BlackBerry, the most popular of these hand-held devices, was developed by Research In Motion (RIM), an Ontario, Canada, firm in 1999. Operated by a trackwheel and tiny buttons, whose resemblance to berry seeds suggested its name, the BlackBerry serves as a mobile telephone, an Internet fax machine, a Web browser, and most recently, a two-way radio. But what has made the Black-Berry indispensable for many businesses is its ability to send and receive e-mail any place that has access to a wireless network. By March 2006 BlackBerry had more than 5.5 million users.

HAND-HELD COMMUNICATION DEVICES SUCH AS THE BLACKBERRY USE COMPUTER TECHNOLOGY. THE BLACKBERRY GOT ITS NAME BECAUSE THE BUTTONS USED TO WORK IT RESEMBLE BERRY SEEDS.

The Global Picture

Until recently, the computer revolution has been staged in highly developed nations, including the United States and Western Europe. In the twenty-first century, this is beginning to change. In 2004 China installed operating systems in more than a million computers and over the next several years plans to install software on 200 million computers.

One way that China and many developing nations can afford this is through the phenomenon of "open source" software. Companies such as Linux, Microsoft's nearest but still distant rival, are making software available at a nominal cost through network connections. Experts predict that operating systems could technically advance developing nations, strengthen domestic economies, and establish their own information technology (IT) networks.

Problems of the Computer Age

As computers shrink the world into a global village with Internet access and connections available to most people, a number of problems have arisen. The advanced capabilities that computers possess can be used for the good of society, but they can also be turned against it. As one advocate agency has pointed out, "the Internet is a useful tool, like a knife, but like a knife, it can also be dangerous."

One of its greatest dangers concerns the welfare of young people. Internet pornography has flourished as an online business since the creation of the World Wide Web (WWW) in 1990. In 1996 the U.S. Congress passed the Communications Decency Act (CDA) in an attempt to restrict children from accessing adult sites, but the Supreme Court ruled that the CDA was unconstitutional the following year. Still, the Internet holds even greater dangers to the young.

According to a survey conducted for the National Center of Missing and Exploited Children (NCMEC), one in seven American youths and teenagers receives a sexual solicitation from someone on the Internet in an average year. Chat rooms and profile Web sites such as MySpace.com are infiltrated by sexual predators, looking for youth of both sexes. By befriending troubled or unsuspecting youth online, some of these predators have gained the young people's confidence and set up meetings that have resulted in molestation, rape, and even murder. Local police and other law enforcement agencies have set up sting operations, with officers posing as youth online to trap predators, but the problem persists. Patrolling the Internet is an awesome and difficult challenge.

Another widespread problem is using computers to invade personal privacy. Unscrupulous individuals and groups use spyware, software designed to intercept or take control of a computer's operations. Spyware, as its name suggests, spies on the user and his or her computer habits. It can take this information and sell it to an ad agency to help it target consumers with e-mail spam and popup ads when the user is online. Other even more intrusive forms of spyware can record users' passwords and even credit card numbers when an individual is making a purchase online. According to one survey, nine out of ten computers connected to the Internet are infiltrated by spyware.

Not all privacy issues originate with unscrupulous Internet criminals. Google and other major search engines routinely collect and store information on users' searches and the computer and browser they used to conduct their searches. Because there are few laws that restrict them from sharing this information with advertisers, the government, and other organizations, the practice can often compromise the users' privacy. In August 2006 America Online (AOL), one of the largest online service providers, posted publicly 20 million Internet search queries made by more than 600,000 customers. Although they quickly removed the postings, the error reverberated through the Web and has been labeled the "Data Valdez" of the search engine industry, referring to the tanker involved in the 1989 Exxon oil spill in Alaska.

To combat this potential problem, some thirty states have enacted breach-notification legislation requiring search engines and other online businesses and agencies to notify users if information they have given is compromised.

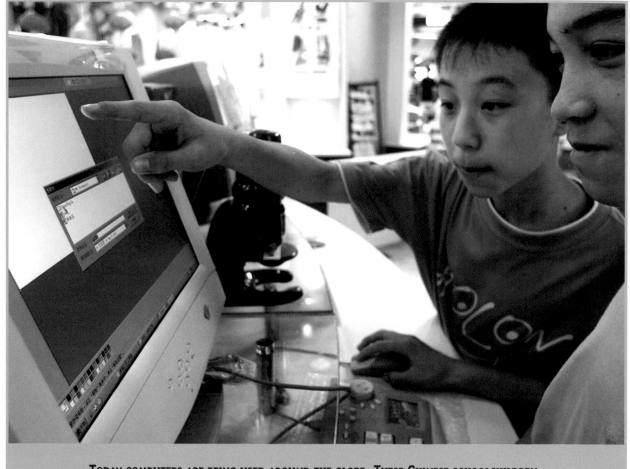

TODAY COMPUTERS ARE BEING USED AROUND THE GLOBE. THESE CHINESE SCHOOLCHILDREN HAVE GATHERED AROUND A COMPUTER IN THEIR CLASSROOM IN BEIJING.

Viruses and Worms

Equally threatening to PCs are viruses, worms, and other so-called mal-mail. Viruses are hidden programs that, once inside a computer, can replicate just as a living virus does and spread through the hardware, deleting data or creating havoc through various malfunctions. Many viruses enter a computer through e-mail. Once the infected e-mail is opened, the virus spreads through the computer's software and will eventually infiltrate the user's address book and mail itself to every person listed. Worms are similar to viruses, but are usually smaller self-contained programs that also invade a computer, self-replicate, and destroy data.

The results of rampant computer viruses and worms can be devastating. The Melissa virus of March 1999 spread so rapidly that major companies affected, including Microsoft, shut down their e-mail systems until the virus could be identified and rooted out. The Mydoom worm caused havoc in 250,000 computers on January 26, 2004. The best defense against spyware, viruses, and worms is protective software that will block an unwanted invader or identify its presence.

While many people use the Internet to steal a person's identity, others, particularly students in high school and college, use it to steal another's words. Plagiarism, always a problem in schools, has reached a new level since the 1990s and the inception of the Internet. Students can copy information from a vast array of sources. There are even Web sites that offer to write term papers and dissertations for a fee. Numerous Web sources are available to identify plagiarism for teachers. Some, such as Plagium, will take a text pasted into a Web box and check it against thousands of articles for repeating word patterns and structures.

While these problems are widespread and not always easily solved, the value of the Internet and computers far outweighs the disadvantages. Just when it seems that we have gone as far as we can go in computer technology, there are new and exciting developments that are just around the corner.

COMPUTERS CAN GO ANYWHERE PEOPLE GO, EVEN TO REMOTE PLACES.

Computing into the Future

The computers of the future are being developed in institutional and commercial laboratories right now. They are being built using the technology of the past and present to usher our world into the future. And what an exciting future it will be.

New Roles for the Personal Computer

Today's PCs are capable of amazing feats, but until recently they mostly functioned independent of other home media and entertainment sources. That has changed. The same wireless network technology that allows every computer in a home or office to work off one modem can make the PC a hub of a home electronics network that will communicate with and control the television, radio, stereo, and DVD player. A wireless relay that can transmit movies, pictures, or streaming video to a television and send music to a stereo was released by Linksys in 2002. Intel has developed PC technology to download television programming similar to systems such as TiVo.

The Incredible Shrinking Computer

The history of the modern computer has featured a continuing reduction in size from the gargantuan models of the 1940s to the streamlined laptops of the 1990s. This reduction was due mostly to the development of

The Semantic Web

You might think after creating the World Wide Web that Tim Berners-Lee would be resting on his laurels. But he's not. In the last few years, he has become immersed in a new Internet project that in its way is just as ambitious as the WWW. He calls it the Semantic Web and, when completed, it may do for databases what the WWW did for Web documents.

"The Semantic Web is a web of data," says Berners-Lee. "There is lots of data we all use every day, and it's not part of the Web. I can see my bank statements on the Web, and my photographs, and I can see my appointments in a calendar. But can I see my photos in a calendar to see what I was doing when I took them? Can I see bank-statement lines in a calendar? Why not? Because we don't have a web of data."

Berners-Lee envisions the Semantic Web as allowing a person to move easily from one database to another for the interchange of information. Databases will be as accessible as Web sites, connected by a linking topic.

The Semantic Web is still a work-in-progress for Berners-Lee and the World Wide Web Consortium that he helps direct. Once completed, he says, this new Web "will connect data I know about with data I never dreaming of using."

PEOPLE OFTEN TURN TO THEIR COMPUTERS FOR NAVIGATIONAL PURPOSES. THESE YOUNG
PEOPLE USE THE CONVENIENCE OF A LAPTOP TO CONFIRM THEIR ROUTE WHILE ON A ROAD TRIP.

the transistor and the microchip. With the advent in the 1990s of nanotechnology and microscopic devices, the shrinking of computers will
continue in the future. Scientists have found that there is virtually no
limit to the number of transistors that can be placed on the atomic
structure of matter. As computer chips get smaller and smaller, a new
world of applications has opened that were never before dreamed of.

The new nanocomputers could be in production in ten to twenty years and will include computers based on electronic, chemical, and mechanical technology. While electronic nanocomputers will perform many of the same kinds of functions as microcomputers do today, only on a much smaller scale, chemical nanocomputers will be able to perform innovative tasks, such as storing and processing data derived directly from nature and the chemical structure of living things. The challenge for bioengineers will be to find a way to get individual atoms and other tiny particles of matter to perform calculations and store data.

Mechanical nanocomputers are the most controversial. The same problems that plagued the first mechanical computer, Charles Babbage's analytical engine, may make the mechanical nanocomputer just as unworkable, depending on how technology evolves in the future.

Scientists at Edinburgh University in Scotland have even begun experimenting with a nanocomputer that can be sprayed on the chests of hospital patients with heart problems. The computer's cells would record the patient's vital signs and then send the data to a larger computer where it can be evaluated.

"At the moment if you want to interface you have to use a keyboard or a mouse, which is very unwieldy," says project head Professor D. K. Arvid. "With this you could take a pen and spray it and it becomes an interface in its own right."

Thinking outside the Computer Box

While nanotechnology is shrinking computer chips to the size of a grain of sand, other developments are expanding the range of computers on a global scale.

In the past, the concept of the computer was usually a contained unit—a huge mainframe, a small PC tower, or a streamlined laptop. The rise of wireless networks has prompted scientists to rethink what a computer is and what it can do. For example, software today does not have to be installed or downloaded into a box, but may be transmitted through wireless networks via fiber optics—the technology of sending data through light carried in transparent fibers. This data can be used,

COMPUTERS HAVE COME A LONG WAY SINCE THE DAYS OF CHARLES BABBAGE'S DIFFERENCE ENGINE. SOME WOULD SAY THAT THE TRUE INNOVATIONS ARE YET TO COME.

THIS COMPUTER FROM THE EARLY 1950S WAS USED BY THE U.S. CENSUS BUREAU TO RECORD AND TALLY POPULATION FIGURES. IMAGINE IF THE PERSONAL COMPUTERS WE USE TODAY WERE THIS LARGE AND UNWIELDY.

as needed, by hundreds of thousands of computer processors in centers around the world. The speed and capability of these networks is mind boggling. One optical fiber can transmit ten billion bits of information in a second.

In September 2005 the iGrid 2005, a supercomputer network workshop, was held at the University of California, San Diego, in La Jolla. Its purpose was to disseminate information about the new "virtual computer" networks and build models for practical applications.

The geographic range of the new "grid computer age" was dramatically demonstrated at the workshop by showing the first high-definition digital video broadcast of an underwater volcanic vent off the coast of the northwestern United States.

"Can you blow up the computer machine room and spread it over the surface of the planet?" asks astrophysicist Larry Smarr, director of the California Institute for Telecommunications and Information Technology. "This is really happening."

Computers have come a long way from the day of ENIVAC when calculating math problems was the ultimate goal. Tomorrow's nanocomputers and virtual computers may help scientists unlock the secrets of the atom and the universe. The computer age is truly a time of wonders.

Time Line

about 1200
The abacus, a device for adding, subtracting, multiplying, and dividing, is adapted and refined in Asia.

1614
Scottish mathematician John Napier perfects a table of numerical symbols called logarithms.

1632
English mathematician William Oughtred invents the slide rule.

1642
French mathematician Blaise Pascal invents the Pascaline, a mechanical calculator.

1673
German Gottfried von Leibniz creates his Leibniz wheel, a machine that can add, subtract, multiply, and divide.

1728
Frenchman Robert Falcon creates punch cards to record a woven pattern.

1801
Joseph-Marie Jacquard uses punch cards to create his Jacquard loom to weave different patterns in cloth.

about 1820
English mathematician Charles Babbage begins work on a difference engine, a computing machine.

1833
Babbage proposes the analytical engine, a predecessor of the modern computer.

1884
American inventor Herman Hollerith creates the first electromechanical computing machine.

1890
Hollerith's computing machines are used to help process results of that year's U.S. census.

1896
Hollerith founds the Tabulating Machine Company.

1924
Computing Tabulating Recording Corporation (CTR) becomes International Business Machines (IBM) Corporation.

1931
American engineer Vannevar Bush invents the differential analyzer.

1937
The Turing machine, a "universal" computer that used symbols instead of letters, is invented by British mathematician Alan Turing.

1943
The Mark I, the first modern computer, is completed by IBM as conceived by physicist Howard Aiken.

1946
John Presper Eckert and John W. Mauchly create ENIAC, the first programmable general-purpose electronic computer.

1947

The first transistor is created at Bell Laboratories in New Jersey by Walter Houser Brattain and John Bardeen.

1952

UNIVAC-I, a new computer by Eckert and Mauchly, correctly predicts Dwight D. Eisenhower as the winner in the presidential election.

1958

The Advanced Research Projects Agency (ARPA) is established to research how computers might be used to compete with Soviet military and space technology.

1959

The first microchip is created by Jack Kilby and Robert Noyce, working independently of each other.

1965

Electronic mail or e-mail is exchanged for the first time between computers.

1969

Ted Hoff, working for Intel, creates the first microprocessor; ARPA begins the Internetting Project to interlink computer networks so they may communicate with each other.

1974

ARPA forms Telenet, the first commercial version of ARPANET for the general public's use.

1975

The Altair 8800, the first home computer, is unveiled by Micro Instrumentation and Telemetry Systems.

Bill Gates and Paul Allen found Microsoft, a computer software company.

1976

Steve Jobs and Steve Wozniak establish Apple Computer Corporation on April 1.

1977

Apple II becomes the first successful personal computer (PC).

1981

IBM comes out with its first PC.

1982

The personal computer is named *Time* magazine's Machine of the Year.

1984

The Apple Macintosh becomes the best-selling PC to date.

1985

Steve Jobs leaves Apple and founds NeXT, a more innovative computer company.

1990

Jobs releases NeXTcube, one of the first "interpersonal computers."

Microsoft Corporation releases Windows 3.0 DOS software that comes to dominate the market.

Tim Berners-Lee, an English computer programmer, develops the World Wide Web near Geneva, Switzerland.

1991

The Apple PowerBook, the first successful laptop computer, appears.

1994

Tim Berners-Lee helps create the World Wide Web Consortium to supervise the Web.

The first blogs, online diaries and journals, appear on the Internet.

1994
The Internet celebrates its twenty-fifth birthday with about 40 million people using it.

1995
The Communications Decency Act (CDA) is passed by Congress to restrict the access of children to adult Web sites.

Programmers at Sun Micro Systems release Java, a pioneering Internet programming language.

Toy Story, the first feature-length entirely computer-animated film, is released in November.

1997
The search engine Google is officially registered by Larry Page and Sergey Brin.

The computer Deep Blue beats chess master Garry Kasparov in a chess tournament.

1999
A hand-held communication device, the BlackBerry, goes on the market.

2001
Wikipedia, the largest online encyclopedia, is launched.

2003
The Can Spam Act is passed by Congress, regulating and reducing spam e-mail.

2004
The Chinese install operating systems (OS) in more than a million computers.

2006

Apple introduces the MacBook Pro, their first Intel microprocessor-based mobile computer.

2007

Microsoft launches Window Vista, their latest consumer operating system.

Glossary

abacus—A device for making mathematical calculations consisting of a frame set with rods on which beads are moved.

bit—A single, basic unit of computer information.

blog—A Web site where users can create diaries or journals to be viewed on the Internet.

bug—A mechanical malfunction in a computer or an error in the software.

byte—A group of bits, usually eight, that are processed as a unit by a computer.

central processing unit (CPU)—The key component of a computer system that contains the circuitry to read and execute program instructions.

chat room—A place on the Internet where any number of users can talk to one another online in real time using text and sometimes photographs, audio, and video.

computer—An electronic device that performs data operations at high speed, according to instructions stored within it.

cursor—A movable symbol used to indicate where data may be input on a computer screen.

debug—To eliminate errors in hardware or software that are stopping a computer from functioning properly.

disk drive—A device in a computer that enables the user to read data from a disk or store data on a disk.

e-mail—A system for sending written messages linked between computers by telecommunications.

Ethernet—A system for exchanging messages between computers on a local-area network.

floppy disk—A round plastic or metal device coated with gamma iron oxide on which computer data or programs is stored.

graphic user interface (GUI)—A software interface on a computer that uses icons, menus, and a mouse to operate instead of typed commands.

hard drive—A disk drive consisting of a rigid disk for storing computer programs and data.

hyperlink—Highlighted words, objects, or graphics in hypertext that link one Web page or site to another.

hypertext—The words or text that appear on a computer screen that are hyperlinks.

integrated circuit (IC)—A circuit of transistors and other components connected on a single wafer or chip in which the components are interconnected to perform a function.

Internet—A large computer network linking smaller computer networks worldwide and allowing them to communicate with one another.

laptop—A small, portable computer.

microchip—A tiny slice of semiconducting material on which a transistor is found.

microprocessor—An integrated computer circuit or chip capable of all the functions of a CPU.

monitor—A component with a display screen for viewing computer data.

mouse—A small device with buttons used to point at and select items on a computer screen.

nanocomputer—A miniaturized computer made up of microscopic devices.

operating system (OS)—The software that directs a computer's operations.

personal computer (PC)—A microcomputer designed for individual use.

program—A series of instructions that enables a computer to perform a task.

random access memory (RAM)—A computer memory used for creating, loading, and viewing programs and temporarily stored data.

search engine—A system that finds World Wide Web pages by looking for specific words or phrases.

server—A computer that makes services available to other computers in a network.

spam—Unsolicited e-mail promoting products and services.

spyware—Software designed to intercept or take control of a computer's operations.

transistor—An electronic device consisting of a semiconductor that can control movement of electricity in a larger electronic device.

uniform resource locator (URL)—A computer address for a feature on the Internet.

virtual reality (VR)—The simulation of a three-dimensional environment that appears real to the individual experiencing it.

virus—A program that can infiltrate a computer and may cause it to malfunction.

Web browser—A software program that will load and display a Web page.

Web page—A single hypertext document on the World Wide Web as appears on a single screen.

Web site—A connected group of pages on the World Wide Web devoted to a single topic or related topics.

World Wide Web (WWW)—A system of interlinked hypertext documents.

worm—A computer code planted illegally in a software program to destroy data in a computer that downloads it.

Web Sites

COMPUTER HISTORY
Computer History Museum
http://www.computerhistory.org

Computer History Time Line
http://www.computerhope.com/history

The History of Computers
http://inventors.about.com/library/blcoindex.htm

INTERNET HISTORY
Living Internet
http://www.livinginternet.com

Explore the Internet
http://smithsonian.yahoo.com/internethistory.html

PERSONAL COMPUTERS
The Obsolete Technology Website
http://oldcomputers.net

TIM BERNERS-LEE AND THE WORLD WIDE WEB
The Official Web site of the World Wide Web Consortium
http://www.w3.org

Bibliography

Books

FOR STUDENTS

Billings, Charlene W. *Supercomputers: Shaping the Future.* New York: Facts on File, 2004.

Gaines, Ann. *Tim Berners-Lee and the Development of the World Wide Web.* Bear, DE: Mitchell Lane Publishers, 2002.

Stewart, Melissa. *Tim Berners-Lee: Inventor of the World Wide Web.* Chicago: Ferguson Publishing Company, 2001.

Sherman, Josepha. *The History of the Internet.* New York: Franklin Watts, 2003.

Tracy, Kathleen. *Marc Andreessen and the Development of the Web Browser.* Bear, DE: Mitchell Lane Publishers, 2002.

FOR TEACHERS

Allan, Roy A. *A History of the Personal Computer: The People and the Technology.* London, Ontario: Allan Publishing, 2001.

Berners-Lee, Tim with Mark Fischetti. *Weaving the Web.* San Francisco: HarperSanFrancisco, 1999.

Ceruzzi, Paul E. *A History of Modern Computing.* Cambridge, MA: MIT Press, 2003.

Laing, Gordon. *Digital Retro: The Evolution and Design of the Personal Computer.* Alameda, CA: Sybex, 2004.

Rheingold, Howard. *Tools for Thought: The History and Future of Mind-Expanding Technology.* Cambridge, MA: MIT Press, 2000.

Wurster, Christian. *Computers: An Illustrated History.* Kölh, Germany: Taschen, 2002.

Index

Page numbers in **boldface** are illustrations.

About the Author

Steven Otfinoski has written more than one hundred and twenty books for young readers. His many biographies include books about Jesse Jackson, Oprah Winfrey, John Wilkes Booth, Nelson Mandela, and Boris Yeltsin. He has also written books on geography, world history, rock music, public speaking, and writing.

He is the author of *Marco Polo: To China and Back, Francisco Coronado: In Search of the Seven Cities of Gold, Vasco Nuñez de Balboa: Discoverer of the Pacific, Juan Ponce de León: Discoverer of Florida,* and *Henry Hudson: In Search of the Northwest Passage* in the Great Explorations series. His other works for Marshall Cavendish include the twelve-volume transportation series for early readers Here We Go! and books on New Hampshire, Georgia, Maryland, and Washington State in the Celebrate the States and It's My State! series.

Two of his books, *Triumph and Terror: The French Revolution* and *Poland: Nation in Transition* were chosen as Books for the Teen Age by the New York Public Library.

Otfinoski is also a produced playwright and has his own theater company History Alive! that brings plays about American history to schoolchildren. He lives with his wife, Beverly, and their two children in Connecticut.